Thrilling Testimonies:
You Shall
Testify

Thrilling Testimonies: You Shall Testify

Wailing Women Worldwide, USA

XULON PRESS

Xulon Press
2301 Lucien Way #415
Maitland, FL 32751
407.339.4217
www.xulonpress.com

© 2023 by Wailing Women Worldwide USA

Foreword by Laide Okafor MD
Foreword by Pastor Michael Obi

FOR INFORMATION:
Wailing Women Worldwide, USA
P.O. Box 655
Hillside, NJ 07205-0655

E-mail: wwusasec@gmail.com
www.wailingwomenworldwideusa.org

All rights reserved solely by the author. The author guarantees all contents are original and do not infringe upon the legal rights of any other person or work.

No part of this book may be reproduced, stored in a retrieval system, or transmitted, in any form or by any means—electronic, mechanical, photocopying, recording, or otherwise—without prior written permission from the Board of Trustees, Wailing Women Worldwide.

Due to the changing nature of the Internet, if there are any web addresses, links, or URLs included in this manuscript, these may have been altered and may no longer be accessible. The views and opinions shared in this book belong solely to the author and do not necessarily reflect those of the publisher. The publisher therefore disclaims responsibility for the views or opinions expressed within the work.

Unless otherwise indicated, Scripture quotations taken from the King James Version (KJV)–public domain.

Scripture quotations taken from the Holy Bible, New International Version (NIV). Copyright © 1973, 1978, 1984, 2011 by Biblica, Inc.™. Used by permission. All rights reserved.

Scripture quotations taken from the Amplified Bible (AMP). Copyright © 1954, 1958, 1962, 1964, 1965, 1987 by The Lockman Foundation. Used by permission. All rights reserved.

Scripture quotations taken from the Holy Bible, New Living Translation (NLT). Copyright ©1996, 2004, 2007 by Tyndale House Foundation. Used by permission of Tyndale House Publishers, Inc.

Paperback ISBN-13: 978-1-6628-7507-6
Ebook ISBN-13: 978-1-6628-7508-3

Table of Contents

Dedication vii
Acknowledgments ix
Forewords xi
Preface xvii

Part One: Christian Obedience 1
   Chapter 1: Consequences of Disobedience 3
   Chapter 2: Being on God's Path 5
   Chapter 3: Obedience Is Better than Sacrifice 11

Part Two: Healing Is the Children's Bread 15
   Chapter 4: God of Impossibility 17
   Chapter 5: God of Infinite Miracles 19
   Chapter 6: Whose Report Will You Believe? 22
   Chapter 7: He Sent His Word and Healed My Disease 24
   Chapter 8: Healed Completely of Breast Cancer 27
   Chapter 9: Jesus Christ Our Healer 28
   Chapter 10: God Is a Great Healer 29
   Chapter 11: God's Uncountable Faithfulness! 31
   Chapter 12: God's Unfailing Love for Me! 34

Part Three: God's Provision 37
   Chapter 13: God's Prophecy Fulfilled 39
   Chapter 14: God's Unfailing Love and Faithfulness 49

Chapter 15: God's Miracle Gift 53
Chapter 16: Trusting God. 55

Part Four: God's Divine Protection 57
Chapter 17: My Grandchildren's Car Accidents 59
Chapter 18: Supernatural Power of God 60
Chapter 19: The Revealer of Secrets!. 63
Chapter 20: The God of Impossibilities: With God, All Things Are
            Possible. 64

Part Five: God's All-Around Faithfulness 65
Chapter 21: My Daughter's Wedding 67
Chapter 22: YAHWEH God Comes to Town! 69
Chapter 23: A New Creation 72
Chapter 24: Wailing Women Worldwide: A Gift from God!. 74
Chapter 25: Incredible God: I Stand in Awe of Him!. 77
Chapter 26: God's Faithfulness 78

Epilogue: Thrilling Testimonies: You Shall Testify 80

Dedication

This book is dedicated to the Holy Spirit, who led and taught us in ways we could never imagine as we undertook this project. All thanks and praise be to God Almighty, for we couldn't have done it without Him.

Acknowledgments

"And they overcame him by the blood of the Lamb and by the word of their testimony, and they did not love their lives to the death" (Rev. 12:11 NKJV).

This book reflects the faith of believers who have recognized the power contained in testimonies. It is a courageous act to be vulnerable and transparent and willingly share what God has done and continues to do in one's life. Yet in penning their testimonies, they have demonstrated their recognition of the unlimited impact these testimonies bring.

These testimonies reveal the heart of genuine Christian disciples to fulfill the Great Commission. We owe a great debt of gratitude to these missionaries and encouragers.

This book could not have been completed without the selfless dedication of the members of the project committee, namely:

- Martina (Tina) Ahonle,
- Bridget Nwachukwu,
- Victoria Uche,
- Onyeka Okafo,
- Lucy Morales, and
- Queensley Udofia.

These servants of the Most High God have dedicated countless hours from conception to completion of this great work. They, without a doubt, exemplified and embodied the meaning of team and teamwork. Thank you, and God bless you.

We would like to express our gratitude to the National Coordinators for your leadership and spiritual oversight. Our final thanks go to the National Project Team for their relentless prayers and Volunteer Editors for the initial editing of the manuscripts.

Pope Saint Paul VI said, "Modern man listens more willingly to witnesses than to teachers, and if he does listen to teachers, it is because they are witnesses."[1] (Pope Paul VI 1975, para. 41).

May the Holy Spirit enable every reader to:

1. Recognize and give praise to God for all the marvelous things He has done and continues to do,
2. Reveal the truth of the gospel of Jesus Christ to those who may be doubting or not yet know Him, and
3. Reveal God's power to touch and change lives.

We ask this in Jesus precious name.
Amen!

Mrs. Yvonne D. Jobe
Wailing Women Worldwide, USA

---

[1] Pope Paul VI. 1975. Evangelii nuntiandi. Apostolic exhortation. Vatican. Accessed March 19, 2023. https://www.vatican.va/content/paul-vi/en/apost_exhortations/documents/hf_p-vi_exh_19751208_evangelii-nuntiandi.html.

Foreword

That which was from the beginning, which we have heard, which we have seen with our eyes, which we have looked upon, and our hands have handled, of the Word of life; (For the life was manifested, and we have seen it, and bear witness, and shew unto you that eternal life, which was with the Father, and was manifested unto us;) That which we have seen and heard declare we unto you, that ye also may have fellowship with us: and truly our fellowship is with the Father, and with his Son Jesus Christ. And these things write we unto you, that your joy may be full (1 John 1:1–4 KJV).

In 2003, the Wailing Women Worldwide movement was established in the United States of America (USA), and since then, we have been gratified to see the Lord our God raise a rapidly growing and formidable army of women interceding for families, the church, and the nation. They are very focused, running to do the Master's will.

The USA National Coordinators' team has the distinction of being the first group of Wailing Women to set up a 24/7 prayer line. Day and night, from different locations in the nation, prayers go up to God concerning the things happening in and around the United States of America.

The testimonies documented in this book are the things heard, seen, and experienced in the lives of individuals and their walk with the Lord in the last two decades. They represent just the tip of the iceberg of heaven's response to prayers and cries from women intercessors. Only in eternity will we get to know the result of the unceasing intercessions that have gone on over time.

> And I saw the seven angels which stood before God; and to them were given seven trumpets. And another angel came and stood at the altar, having a golden censer; and there was given unto him much incense, that he should offer it with the prayers of all saints upon the golden altar which was before the throne. And the smoke of the incense, which came with the prayers of the saints, ascended up before God out of the angel's hand. And the angel took the censer, and filled it with fire of the altar, and cast it into the earth: and there were voices, and thunderings, and lightnings, and an earthquake (Rev. 8:2–5 KJV).

The Bible is a book of testimonies. As we study it, we see men and women in different dispensations tell of their encounters with God and how He intervened in situations to bring deliverance, healing, and mindset change, and led many to positively affect society and fulfill their destinies. It tells of successes and failures, rebukes and encouragements, lessons learned, and unlearned habits. It is a book of practical wisdom, which we can apply to daily life in every nation.

Paraphrasing Dr. Mike Bagwell, the last chapter of the Acts of the Apostles is open-ended and has no closing remark. Our own stories and experiences are the continuation of the Acts of the Holy Spirit in our time. As you would readily admit, these testimonies are real and constitute proof of God's existence and His involvement and intervention in our lives.

The testimonies in this book are told in simple language, and one can identify with the everyday situations the authors narrated. You will easily identify with those who had a need for healing and comfort, and the need to get accurate directions, make the right decisions, and take the right turns.

It tells of the results of trusting God to answer prayers, taking a leap of faith in the dark, obeying God's promptings even when things look bleak, and eventually, finding light at the end of the tunnel.

God encourages us to keep records of His dealings with us and leaves this as evidence to future generations. This is what the Wailing Women (USA) have begun to do through the compilation of these wonderful testimonies. We should not underestimate the power of testimonies. They not only strengthen and boost our faith, but they also serve as an encouragement to those contemplating the next steps to take. They are a powerful tool to bring others to the saving knowledge of the great God, whom we love and serve. Through our testimonies, we overcome Satan and his cohorts.

> "And they overcame him by the blood of the Lamb, and by the word of their testimony; and they loved not their lives unto the death" (Rev. 12:11 KJV).

As you read the testimonies penned down in this book, may they help to deepen your personal relationship with God, bolster your faith, and encourage you to know that God is not afar off; He is near, and He can be touched with the feelings of our infirmities. He responds when we call upon Him.

Get copies for your family and friends!

Dr. Mrs. Laide Okafor
Head International Coordinator,
Wailing Women Worldwide

Foreword

"This beginning of miracles did Jesus in Cana of Galilee and manifested forth his glory; and his disciples believed on him" (John 2:11 KJV).

For thirty years, Jesus prepared for His assignment of destiny on earth, and as He was baptized, the heavens opened, and God sealed His Son with the power of the Holy Spirit. It was not until this marriage at Cana that the evidence of this power distinguished Him and confirmed to His disciples that He was ordained of God.

The Wailing Women Worldwide has a mandate that is exceptionally peculiar in its calling: to demonstrate the discipline of prayer, the mindset of spiritual warriors, and the power of breakthrough prayers, as had happened with Jesus in the above Scripture, where, after much training, there was the manifestation/evidence of authority and power through the miracles. I believe your life will never be the same after reading the Wailing Women's amazing testimonies of miraculous breakthroughs in different aspects and areas of life's battles. They have revived and provoked my faith that God has never changed; He still answers prayers and is a miracle worker.

I don't know how best to encourage and inspire anyone going through some difficult times or impossible situations than to recommend this book of testimonies. Faith comes by hearing and hearing the testimonies of breakthrough prayers and the faithfulness of God through these precious Wailing Women.

Pastor Michael Okwuosah Obi
Executive Director/National Coordinator,
African Strategic Leadership Prayer Network (ASLPN)

Preface

Thrilling Testimonies: You Shall Testify

The Wailing Women Worldwide, USA (aka Women Intercessors for the Church and the Nations), received a prophetic word some years ago to declare, "I am not serving the Lord in vain!" God instructed that we write and paste this declaration in strategic places in our homes where we can see it often and voice it out. Those who understand the power of the spoken word, who are also obedient, obeyed the instruction. It has been a popular maxim in Wailing Women USA since then. As we declare it, we keep seeing its fruit in our lives and families.

The Lord also tells us, "You shall testify!" He is not done with us yet. He keeps doing beautiful things in our lives and multiplying those testimonies in the lives of those who hear them. Indeed, we are not serving the Lord in vain. Everyone who serves him faithfully has a beautiful story to tell of his faithfulness and unfailing love. The Lord is ever faithful to His Word. He says, "I the Lord do not change. So you, the descendants of Jacob, are not destroyed" (Mal. 3:6).

This compilation and publication of the various acts of God in the lives of our members, titled *Thrilling Testimonies: You Shall Testify*, is the fulfillment of the Scripture: "So shall my word be that goeth forth out of my mouth: it shall not return unto me void, but it shall accomplish that which I please, and it shall prosper in the thing whereto I sent it" (Isa. 55:11 KJV).

God is blessing us in the three dimensions of wealth, health, and soul. As it is written, "Beloved, I wish above all things that thou mayest prosper and be in health, even as thy soul prospereth" (3 John 1:2 KJV). Brethren, key into the testimonies and hold on to God for the fulfillment of His promises in your life, and you shall also testify.

Read, savor, enjoy, and believe in the Lord your God, as it is written, "So shall ye be established; believe his prophets, so shall ye prosper" (2 Chron. 20:20b KJV). Amen!

Editing Team
Wailing Women Worldwide, USA

Part One

CHRISTIAN OBEDIENCE

Chapter 1

Consequences of Disobedience

"And Samuel said, Hath the Lord as great delight in burnt offerings and sacrifices, As in obeying the voice of the Lord? Behold, to obey is better than sacrifice, And to hearken than the fat of rams" (1 Sam. 15:22 KJV).

On the day I migrated from Nigeria to New Jersey, United States of America, my family organized a send-forth prayer for me. On that fateful day, a seven-year-old girl who had no idea about my intended journey to the United States prophesied into my life, saying: ***"When you get to where you are going, never will you do two jobs, and you will do work for God."*** She said this, crying and pleading with me.

Upon arrival in the USA, I got a job at a nursing home where I was in charge of the pastoral unit, conducting Bible studies for the residents. It was full-time employment, but I decided to get a second job elsewhere. I then decided to make my first job at the nursing home part-time and the second job, which was in a group home, full-time. The first has become last and last first.

It happened that the second job became a torment and torture for me. The young administrator was inconsiderate and a thorn in my flesh with her assignments and demands. The things she demanded of me were annoying and had nothing to do with my job description. I hated the job.

One day, I was returning from my full-time job to go to my part-time when a limo taxi driver struck my car, and it landed upside down on I-78 in New Jersey. While lying inside the car, I was praying to God to give me a second chance. "Then Jonah prayed unto the Lord his God out of the fish's belly" (Jon. 2:1 KJV).

When the police arrived, they cut the car, brought me out, and took me to the nearest hospital, Overlook Hospital, in New Jersey. I was in great pain at the hospital for three days.

Upon discharge from the hospital, I went back to my first job at the nursing home, conducting Bible studies, on full-time employment. I forever jettisoned the idea of a second job.

At the end of the year, when I filed my tax return with the Internal Revenue Service (IRS), I was made to refund $6,000.00 for making too much money.

Through the accident and loss to the IRS, I learned that there are consequences for disobedience. It is very important to note that only prompt and complete obedience is acceptable to God.

Many of the residents at the nursing home had given their lives to God through the Bible study sessions. To God be the glory, and many of these individuals went home with the Lord during this period of the COVID-19 outbreak. "Precious in the sight of the Lord is the death of his saints" (Ps. 116:15 KJV).

Mrs. Roseline Ngozi Ojefua,
Wailing Women Worldwide, USA

Chapter 2

Being on God's Path

I was raised in a religious way, which made me involved in most activities my church organized for my age group from childhood, such as Anglican Children's Ministry, Girls' Brigade, and Anglican Youth Fellowship. My godly upbringing positioned me to serve God from childhood, but I did not know Him. I even lived in a church compound with my grandparents at an early stage in life. But this did not prevent me from involving myself in all the vices other children and youths were involved in. The only difference was that I did them in secret because of my conservative background. But then, I did not have peace because I had not surrendered my life to Christ.

A time came when I felt a vacuum in my life. None of those religious activities could fill this vacuum. There was a group of people I envied; they were the born-again Christians, the real Christians. There was an aura of peace and purity around them. At a certain point, I wanted to join them. But I was not ready to part with my lifestyle and friends then. So, I kept away.

I knew the truth, having read and heard the Word of God, but I was not willing to make the sacrifice. Little did I know that none of those reasons were worth my spending eternity in hell fire. God was waiting and watching. And I knew that my born-again elder sister and my parents were praying for me.

Then on that fateful day when I could delay no longer, I was the one who reminded others of the fellowship time and did not want to be late. I could not wait to meet with God. It was the year I entered the university, and it was my first day attending a fellowship on campus as an undergraduate. I cannot remember the words of the preacher in the meeting that day. I was anxiously waiting for the call to surrender my life to Jesus Christ. When that call was made, I rushed out and received the Lord Jesus as my personal Lord and Savior. I was born again. **I made up my mind not to settle for mediocrity.** That day was November 1, 1987, at the Arts Theater University of Nigeria, Nsukka. My life had turned around.

I was spiritually hungry and cried out to God for a filling. Within two weeks, I was baptized with the Holy Ghost with the evidence of speaking in tongues. I have enjoyed my walk with the Lord ever since.

I have neither been strong nor perfect, but the unseen hand of the Almighty God has sustained me. If anything, I desire to be nearer to Him now than when I first believed. Even the "mighty men" have backslid, but He has upheld me. He is indeed a covenant-keeping God. I owe everything to Him—my life, joy, peace, academic attainment, successful marriage, children, and so on. I gained everything good and lost everything bad (including hellfire) when I surrendered my life to the Lord. I cannot imagine what my life would have been without Him. I am so happy to be His witness. Lasting joy can only be found in Jesus Christ.

From the time I surrendered my life to Christ, I have desired to be fruitful because I believed God had a purpose for me, even though I did not understand it initially.

One Sunday after service in my church in Enugu, Nigeria, I saw a flyer about women gathering in Port Harcourt, Nigeria, to pray, and I instantly connected in my spirit to the move. I thought, "This is the kind of place I want to be." But then, I felt I was already busy with my church fellowship, Evangelical Fellowship in the Anglican Communion (EFAC), and Full Gospel Businessmen's Fellowship, so I did not attend that meeting.

Years later, a friend invited me to join Wailing Women Enugu, but I still responded that I did not have time for that. The right reaction would have been to pray about it, but I did not. Sometimes we are too busy working for God that we do not pay attention to what He wants us to do. But God patiently waited for me, and around 2004, I decided to attend their meeting, just to visit. I did not intend to be a member at the time.

In this meeting, I sensed the presence of God so much. I had been a Christian for some years, but I had never attended a meeting so saturated with the tangible presence of God, especially as they praised God. Yet the members were ordinary laywomen. What I saw there magnetized me to the group. From that day, I never missed the monthly general meeting again.

After a while, another friend invited me to start attending the lowest-level coordinators' meeting (the mobilizers) even though I had not been made a coordinator. In their meeting, I saw a higher level of God's divine presence than the one I experienced in the general meetings. I saw the Holy Spirit expose a lady, a member of the group, who did not join in the one-week fasting the group had at the time, and it left me speechless. I have not forgotten the experience. I understood the gathering to be so holy that you could not toy with sin because the Holy Spirit would expose you. Wow! I thought, "This is the place to be." I felt the Spirit of God say to me, "If you like what you saw, dive deeper or come up higher." Of course, I liked it, so I began to regularly attend the mobilizers' weekly meetings.

Usually, at this level, they organize an interview for those who have been consistent and committed members to make them coordinators. The purpose of the interview is to ascertain that you are genuinely born again, spirit-filled, and available for the work.

I was invited to a three-day shut-in retreat for all coordinators; however, I still had not gone through the coordinator interview process, so technically, I was not a coordinator. In this retreat, anyone who joins is not permitted to leave the venue until the end of the three days. There were good reasons for me not to be there. One, I was not a coordinator. Second, my children were young, and their father was in the US. However, on the second day of the retreat, God asked about me and asked them to bring me. I came and stayed outside. They invited me in, organized a quick personal interview for me, and anointed me as a coordinator.

According to the leaders, God saw that I ought to be a coordinator and sent for me. This experience made me fear God even more. In one of the coordinators' night vigils, God said He would send some of us abroad to work for him. I did not think I would be one of them. But after some time, God spoke to me to go to the United States. It was difficult because I loved my job, and I had a particularly good and promising position. I told God that getting a US visa was difficult, but He told me He would surprise me through the way He would work it out.

And that was exactly what happened. The visa interview was amazingly easy. They did not request the usual documents from me but merely asked why I wanted to travel. I told them I wanted to participate in the 2011 Wailing Women Worldwide USA National Conference. They asked me what Wailing Women was about, and I explained the vision. They gave me a two-year multiple entries visa. It was a miracle because I had twice applied for a US visa for other reasons, but they did not give it to me.

When I got the visa, God spoke to me through a prophetic voice, "Go and gather women and tell them about wailing!" I came for the conference, managed to share the vision of Wailing Women with a few ladies I met, and returned to Nigeria and my job. I came again to the US the following year (January 2012) and told God, "If you truly want me to stay back, I do not want to stay one day in this country as an illegal alien." My husband was not even in the position to file papers for me, but we prayed and sought the service of an immigration lawyer while dedicating myself to the assignment God gave me to gather women and tell them about wailing.

Another miracle happened when God gave me permanent residence before my visa expired. **When we are determined to obey God, He handles the obstacles.**

Today, my life revolves around serving God in Wailing Women Worldwide because that is where God called me to be. I do not count the time I put into this work. Only God knows, and He is a good pay Master. I received one instruction from Him, and I am trying my best to fulfill it.

If He sends me to another country tomorrow, I will go there because He said to me, "Just follow me!" Sometimes it looks humanly stupid. It makes no sense to leave one of the best jobs in Nigeria and do God's work. Nevertheless, at His demand, I am doing it and am determined to follow Him to the end.

God has used my encounter with the move of Wailing Women Worldwide to impact my life extraordinarily, accelerating my spiritual growth. I have experienced Him as a real God who loves, listens, speaks, guides, and directs. He is very much involved in the lives of His followers. He is nearer to me than I was made to believe before I joined this movement. I am so grateful to God that He has given me a platform to fulfill my calling as an intercessor with heavily anointed and God-fearing leaders as my example. I do not have to labor alone.

Song:
When He Calls Me I Will Answer
Eduardo J. Lango, Hymnary

> When He calls me, I will answer (3 times)
> I'll be somewhere working for my Lord
> I'll be somewhere, working (3 times)
> Working for my Lord[2]

Mrs. Nwabuogo Okafo,
Wailing Women Worldwide, USA

---

[2] Lango, Eduardo J. "I'll Be Listening." In Lead Me, Guide Me, second edition, hymn number 620. GIA Publications, 1987

Chapter 3

Obedience Is Better than Sacrifice

After working for sixteen years around the clock in an odd time shift, on weekends, and so forth, I started praying to God to provide me with a job that would enable me to serve Him more. The burden was so great that I was so inspired to **run for the Lord**. I prayed without giving up like the persistent widow in Luke 18:1–8. Then my job became so overwhelming that even a promotion was denied. My credentials were intimidating to the management.

I continued building my portfolio and praying, knowing that man may block the way, but God opens at His time. I would also refer to God's Word, "Blessed are ye, when men shall revile you, and persecute you, and shall say all manner of evil against you falsely, for my sake" (Matt. 5:11 KJV).

It got to the point where I started looking for a position outside my organization. I even placed my resignation before I was offered a new job. Then came the offer from my King of kings. I got the perfect job that created room to serve the Lord In this job, when it snows, on holidays, and on weekends, I have off. What a great room made by the Lord.

At the beginning of each year, I take time to be silent and hear from the Lord. In 2019, two years into the job, the Lord ministered to me to find a vibrant fellowship and serve Him more. I now know that Wailing Women have been praying for God to bring in women to serve God concerning the mandate in Jeremiah 9:17. God says, "Consider now! Call for wailing women to come . . . call for wailing women" (NIV).

I called my classmate in Kansas State to give me contact details for a Full Gospel businessmen fellowship, and my classmate referred me to a wailer coordinator from Nigeria who was staying in Canada to nurse her daughter through the delivery of her baby. The wailer directed me to call a wailer in Maryland. I called and left messages multiple times but received no response. I did not relent because it was in obedience to the Lord. I called back the wailer in Canada like the persistent widow until she gave me the Maryland PG chapter leader's number. As soon as I called, she responded and gave me a rundown of Wailing Women in Maryland and their fellowship time. I started with the 24/7 online prayer line and attended in person the PG Chapter fellowship, where the chapter leader warmly welcomed me.

Fortunately, my son graduated the following month from college, and the chapter leader showed up at the celebration with two days' notice and prayed at the celebration.

I continued fellowship with the brethren and was engaged in evangelism and welfare outreach. That same year 2019, I attended my first conference in Baltimore, Maryland, my state of residence (God's plan). Wailing Women, your prayers have not been in vain. The Holy Spirit sought me and relocated me into God's vineyard, where I can do exploits for the Lord.

Great changes have befallen me, or should I say, reaching **higher ground** since worshiping God with Wailing Women. I pray, worship, and go around using the slightest opportunity to help people come to Christ after joining Wailing Women.

During the pandemic, I evangelized so much through the phone. We have all it takes and the resources we need to help people turn back to Christ, our Lord and Savior. In my church, by the power of the Holy Spirit, my church members call on me for intercessory prayer without my volunteering. I have preached in the pulpit on intercessory prayer for one another. Everything has turned around for my good.

I prepare myself to be always ready because we do not know the day or the hour. Thank God for our international coordinators who obeyed God for this movement to be made manifest. Now we worship in God's beauty of holiness. Have we thought about how worship in heaven will be?

Through God's grace, I serve on five committees in Wailing Women USA. It might seem like much, but I cannot complain. Remember, *I needed to serve the Lord more*. I have invited six sisters who come on the prayer line; two of the sisters are actively moderating on the 24/7 prayer line and have associated themselves in chapter meetings. The rest have attended the 24/7 prayer line but need to yield themselves as the Holy Spirit is already working.

Adhering to the Holy Spirit's instructions, I was able to invite a friend to the conference, and she, in turn, invited her friend. God wants us to fetch every woman back to Himself.

This is just a token of what He has been doing within a small amount of time in my life. There are numerous breakthroughs that I will save for the next volume of our testimony book. People of God, the harvest is full, looking for laborers like you and me. Let us keep the ball rolling and labor for the Lord, for it will be the sweetest moment to be in heaven together and enjoy eternity. The Lord is good. I will lift Him higher anywhere I go. I will lift God higher.

Victoria Uche,
Wailing Women Worldwide, USA

Part Two

Healing Is the Children's Bread

EXODUS 15:26

Chapter 4

God of Impossibility

"And Jesus looking upon them saith, with men it is impossible, but not with God: for with God all things are possible" (Mark 10:27 KJV).

In August 2018, I went to the Wailing Women International Conference/Medical Mission at Port Harcourt, Nigeria, and left my wonderful and lovely husband at home in good health. On August 11, 2018, he became ill while I was still away, and my brother took him to the hospital. At the hospital, his heart rate was so high that he was intubated (placed on life support) in the emergency room and later sent to the intensive care unit for observation. His condition deteriorated to a critical level that all hope was lost, and brethren were frequenting the hospital for prayers.

Upon arrival to the USA from Nigeria, I was asked to extubate him (pull the plug) and let him die. I told them no and that God would turn him around. I held onto God's Word and never gave up. "But e was wounded for our transgressions, he was bruised for our iniquities: the chastisement of our peace was upon him; and with his stripes, we are healed" (Isa. 53:5 KJV).

I kept an all-night vigil at his bedside, calling on the name of Jehovah Rapha. God did answer me and the prayers offered by the saints. God turned my husband around. "Say unto them, As truly as I live, saith the Lord, as ye have spoken in mine ears, so will I do to you" (Num. 14:28 KJV).

When my husband was extubated, a series of tests were conducted, and it was discovered that his gastroenterologist had wrongfully placed a pancreatic stent (tube), which had caused sepsis (extreme response to infection). God sent an experienced and God-fearing doctor who was able to successfully remove the stent (tube). Immediately, the fever subsided, he got better, and was discharged.

Since then, my husband has not been to the hospital, and he has been enjoying divine health meant for the Lord's children. "But he answered and said, It is not meet to take the children's bread, and to cast *it* to dogs" (Matt. 15:26 KJV).

I learned through this ordeal that God is faithful and not to give up in praying and trusting God. There is no situation or circumstances He cannot turn around. Glory to God for the great things He has done.

> "Except the LORD build the house, they labor in vain that build it: Except the LORD keep the city, the watchman waketh *but* in vain" (Ps. 127:1 KJV).

Mrs. Roseline Ngozi Ojefua,
Wailing Women Worldwide, USA

Chapter 5

God of Infinite Miracles

"It is of the Lord's mercies that we are not consumed, because his compassions fail not. They are new every morning: Great is thy faithfulness" (Lam. 3:22–23 KJV).

Song:
Every Time I Turn Around
Yaw Osei-Owusu

> Every time I turn around,
> God keeps blessing me.
> Every time I turn around,
> God keeps blessing me.
> Every time I turn around,
> God keeps blessing me.
> Hallelujah. Amen.
> God keeps blessing me.[3]

---

[3] Yaw Osei-Owusu. "Every Time I Turn Around." Every Time I Turn Around. Amazon Music, 2021. Streaming audio

I have seen the Lord's goodness, mercy, and compassion in my life. The Lord has been good to me and my family, so I will pick three out of many testimonies to share with you.

1. *Miracle of Salvation*

My greatest testimony is having the Lord as my Lord and Savior. "For when we were yet without strength, in due time Christ died for the ungodly. For scarcely for a righteous man will one die, yet peradventure for a good man some would even dare to die. But God commanded his love toward us, in that, while we were yet sinners, Christ died for us" (Rom. 5:6–8 KJV).

2. *Healing Testimonies*

The Lord healed me many times because He is the Lord who heals me. When the enemy comes in like a flood to overpower my soul and body, the Lord always lifts a standard against him. The Bible says that He sent His Word, and He healed them (Exod. 15:26 KJV). His Word has always healed me.

3. *Healed of Lupus*

I was diagnosed with lupus in 1998 and was hospitalized for a few days. I was told there was no cure and that I would not live more than fifteen years from diagnosis due to the progression of the disease. I refused the diagnosis and declared to the doctors that my expectation was to be healed, and I would believe God's Word and claim healing for my body. Even though I was placed on medication for life, I told the Lord He would have to deliver me from this medication because of the side effects of using the medication long term.

On December 31, 1999, during the crossover prayer, I asked the Lord to help me get off the medication because I believe He had healed me. When I finally went to sleep that night, I was visited in my sleep and saw a figure from the bottom of his skirts, the hem of his garment. Immediately, I felt touched and healed and started singing from my sleep, "I have touched the hems of his garment, I have touched the hems of his garment; He has made me whole."

My husband was already awake and heard me singing from my sleep and asked me why. I said I was healed. I stopped my medication, and the Lord sustained me. I still do blood work every six months until now, and my last blood work showed no trace of the disease. "Say unto them, As truly as I live, saith the LORD, as ye have spoken in mine ears, so will I do to you" (Num. 14:28 KJV). Praise the Lord!

Healed of Kidney Failure

My kidneys were failing, and my doctor was concerned. The test result was about 59 eGFR (estimated glomerular filtration rate), and he told me that there was usually no cure. He said to drink lots of water and exercise regularly. I went to the Lord in prayer because I didn't want to be put on dialysis. The Lord told me to start using the bitter leaves that I was growing in my backyard. He gave me more ingredients to add to it, so I used organic products to make smoothies every day for six months. By my next appointment, my blood work showed that my kidneys went up to 97 eGFR. Glory to God in the highest!

Ebun Adeyemi,
Wailing Women Worldwide, USA

Chapter 6

Whose Report Will You Believe?

"I am the LORD, The God of all mankind. Is anything too hard for me?" (Jer. 32:27 NIV).

God Delivered My First Son from Death

The Lord called me into Wailing Women Worldwide (WWW) in 2010. In late 2010, my oldest son, while in medical school, started having problems with double vision. He went for a medical checkup and was diagnosed with myasthenia gravis. The doctor told him that people with this diagnosis do not last but about five months. Our family was shattered, and my son was devastated, so I took my husband to the inner court of the Most High God. Like King Hezekiah, I laid the case of my son completely out.

From childhood, the Lord had called and equipped me to be a facilitator. By the grace of God, I delighted myself in giving to the needy and supporting widows and orphans. I remembered so vividly telling the Lord that if there must be death, it could not be any one of mine because that was NOT one of His promises for His faithful followers. After taking my case to the court of heaven, we left the petition in the holy temple of the Lord God Almighty.

We flew our son, who was in Florida, to our home in Houston that night. The doctor in Florida referred us to another specialist in Houston. At the doctor's office here in Houston, they reviewed the images/ultrasounds that were done in Florida. He was requested to repeat the tests in Houston, and he did. The bombshell: the doctor could not see anything they had seen in Florida.

For those who do not know, myasthenia gravis disease (a condition caused by a breakdown in communication between nerves and muscles) involves a small organ in the body that completes its function before the age of ten years and stays dormant in the body.

The doctor advised the organ to be removed, and they did.

My son takes a small dose of medication now, but I am trusting the Lord that before this book is published, the Almighty God would have completely healed him, and the medication discontinued for good.

I trust my King and Lord, Jehovah Rapha.

Curtis Ndubuisi Okpara
Polished Arrow, Wailing Women Worldwide, USA

Chapter 7

He Sent His Word and Healed My Disease

"He sent forth His word and healed them, And delivered them from their destruction" (Ps. 107:20 KJV).

"O Lord, I cried unto thee, and thou hast healed me" (Ps. 30:2 KJV).

As a young girl, I desired to become an entrepreneur and start my enterprise. My father was a successful businessperson, and I was fortunate to have exposure to the world of business through my father's business endeavors.

To achieve my goal as an entrepreneur, I sold an array of foods as a way of producing a stream of income to help my family while developing skills to start my business.

I initially had planned to study accounting. However, when we moved to the United States from Nigeria, I decided to enter the nursing field when I saw how understaffed the hospitals were and the opportunity to take care of the sick, especially having recently lost my beloved father after a long-term illness.

I was thrilled when I discovered that I could combine my nursing skills with my dream of starting my own business. However, what I did not anticipate was the challenge of running a business, taking care of my family, and holding down a part-time job to make ends meet as I waited for my business to become profitable.

I had not prayed to God or consulted with Him about His plan and direction for my life, physical health, and business ventures.

One day while performing my regular daily activities, I experienced anxiety, excessive perspiration, an increased heart rate, and an increase in blood pressure reading. During an examination with my physician, I received the diagnosis of hypertension and hyperthyroidism. The physician discussed two options to consider for treating my hyperthyroidism, either surgery or iodine treatment.

After weighing the two, I opted for the iodine treatment, which now put everything in reverse. I went from hyperthyroidism to hypothyroidism. At first, it looked like everything was okay, but over time, the toll of not being able to produce thyroid hormones became evident. I started feeling sluggish, sleepy, and forgetful. These symptoms were an embarrassment at times.

I started taking Synthroid, and that medication came with its own set of side effects. It was at this point that I cried out to the Lord for healing. I would omit taking the Synthroid medication. Instead, I prayed and fasted, putting my faith to work and hoping for God's healing of my physical condition.

After not taking my medication for a couple of days, my symptoms returned with a vengeance. I did not know what else to do. Then in 2016, I attended Wailing Women Worldwide Leadership Summit in Ethiopia. The leadership summit was about healing.

Our spiritual mother, Mama Ebele, told us she was convinced that God wanted to heal His people during this summit. That night, she led us to study the book of Luke, which spoke about the healings that Christ performed. After we studied the Bible, we prayed to God for healing. At that point, I decided to hold off on the medication, once again, hoping for healing.

Several days after not taking my medication, I had trouble breathing. But I thought it was due to the high altitude in Ethiopia. I took the medication, but I felt guilty because I felt I did not have the faith to experience the healing power of God. I remember going into the bathroom and repenting before the Lord. Afterward, as I opened up my Bible to read, the Lord took me to 1 Samuel 2:9. I was made to understand from the Bible verse that it was not by the arm of flesh that I would receive my healing but at the timing and season of the Holy Spirit. *After this revelation, I had peace.* I now understood that **God would do it in His own time and not my own.** "For by strength shall no man prevail" (1 Sam. 2:9b KJV).

On my way home from the summit, I clearly heard the Lord in my spirit give me Bible verses for healing, telling me to go on a three-day fast. When I got home, I recited the Bible verses the Lord gave me and went on a three-day fast. I have not taken Synthroid medication nor felt ill effects since the summit in the year 2016.

I give God the glory and honor for healing my thyroid condition. It was God who healed me, and Him alone. He sent His Word and healed my disease.

Margaret Oge Ukatu,
Wailing Women Worldwide, USA

Chapter 8

Healed Completely of Breast Cancer

But I will restore you to health and heal your wounds,' declares the LORD" (Jer. 30:17 NIV).

I found lumps in my breasts in March 2019, two months after I had a total knee replacement surgery on December 11, 2018. A mammogram and biopsy performed confirmed that I had a high grade of infiltrating carcinoma stage two, running at the rate of 88 percent (aggressive type). I told the doctor that cancer cannot outrun God.

I had aggressive chemotherapy treatments, lost all my hair and appetite, my immune system was down, and I was weak. I prayed, listened to inspirational worship songs, and stood on God's healing Scriptures. The Lord Jesus gave me peace through my ordeal, and I was overwhelmed by the Holy Spirit's powerful healing touch. My God was faithful. I had mastectomy surgery, followed by radiation and more chemotherapy. All treatments ended on January 20, 2021, and my prognosis was so amazing.

God healed me through the healing power of Jesus Christ. Now I am completely cancer free. I am eternally grateful to God, my heavenly Father. Jesus is and will always be the Lord of my life.

Abigail Oikelome,
Wailing Women Worldwide, USA

Chapter 9

Jesus Christ Our Healer

"But I will restore you to health and heal your wounds declares the Lord" (Jer. 30:17 NIV).

Years ago, my young cousin lived with me when she was in high school. Daily, we had our family prayer altar in the morning and at bedtime. As a young girl, I had the opportunity of presenting the gospel of Jesus Christ to her and often used current events to minister and demonstrate Christ's power as God afforded me such an opportunity.

One time, a boil developed on one of my fingers. I showed it to her during our family prayer, and we prayed for God's healing overnight. The next morning, I woke up with a pain-free and boil-free finger. The growth dried up as we prophesied over it the night before. I was able to show and prove to my cousin that God's answer to prayers can be faster than expected and that He is our healer. She said to me, "Aunty, this is a clear-cut miracle." She believed me that Jesus is indeed our healer.

Jesus Christ, our Jehovah Rapha, has the power to heal us in any situation—physically, emotionally, mentally, and spiritually. To Him be the glory. Blessings.

Josephine Nwoko,
Wailing Women Worldwide

Chapter 10

God Is a Great Healer

> "If you diligently heed the voice of the Lord your God and do what is right in His sight, give ear to His commandments and keep all His statutes, I will put none of the diseases on you which I have brought on the Egyptians. For I am the Lord who heals you" (Exod.15:26 KJV).

Prayer changes things! My husband's caregiver asked for prayer about a year ago, believing in the words of Philippians 4:6 (NIV): "Do not be anxious about anything, but in everything by prayer and supplication with thanksgiving let your requests be made know to God." Her husband was diagnosed with cancer of the lungs/upper stomach and went through chemotherapy.

I presented the prayer request to our Indiana Wailing Women Worldwide Chapter, and we prayed for her husband. According to Matthew 7:7 (KJV), "Ask and it will be given to you: seek and you will find: knock and the door will be opened to you." Brethren gathered and prayed according to James 5:16 (NIV): "Therefore, confess your sins to each other and pray for each other so that you may be healed. The prayer of a righteous person is powerful and effective."

A few months later, her husband contracted COVID-19 and had a chest X-ray. The family grieved over the infection. "And we know that all things work together for good to them that love God, to them who are the called according to his purpose" (Rom. 8:28 KJV). The X-ray showed no cancer in his lungs and upper stomach as previously diagnosed. The doctor couldn't believe it. "But God hath chosen the foolish things of the world to confound the wise; and God hath chosen the weak things of the world to confound the things which are mighty" (1 Cor. 1:27 KJV). He referred them to a specialist for more tests.

My husband's caregiver called on May 7, 2021, to tell us that her husband was **cancer free!**

We, the unprofitable servants of the Wailing Women Worldwide Indiana Chapter, are grateful that God has used us to showcase His healing power on the caregiver's husband. "So likewise, ye, when ye shall have done all those things which are commanded you, say, We are unprofitable servants: we have done that which was our duty to do" (Luke 17:10 KJV).

Glory to God for honoring His Word, which says, "Who his own self bare our sins in his own body on the tree, that we, being dead to sins, should live unto righteousness: by whose stripes ye were healed" (1 Pet. 2:24 KJV).

> "Rejoice always, pray continually, give thanks in all circumstances: for this is God's will for you in Christ Jesus" (1 Thess. 5:16–18 NIV). I conclude to testify, "So if the Son sets you free, you will be free indeed" (John 8:36 NIV).

Che'rie Keesling,
Wailing Women Worldwide

Chapter 11

God's Uncountable Faithfulness!

I have many testimonies, but I cannot tell it all. Our God is great, He is so loving and kind, and His mercy is from everlasting to everlasting. To Him be all the glory!

Since I gave my life to Christ, God has been fighting my battles.

In Nigeria, around 2011, I used to have a strange kind of fever or illness that I could not explain. Sometimes I would fast and pray about it, but one early morning, I heard the voice of God speaking to me, "**All your sickness has gone to Egypt**." I believed it and claimed it, and I was healed. Since then, whenever I feel sick, I remind the Lord, "Father, you told me that all my sickness has gone to Egypt, and I will be healed." I pray the same prayer when I have arthritis pain in my leg, and I will lay my hand on the area where I have the pain and remind God of His promises. God heals me!

Secondly, God delivered me from the spirit of fear and unbelief, by which the enemy tried to steal my life. The Word of God says, "My people are destroyed for lack of knowledge" (Hosea 4:6 KJV). I thank God for His mercy and love. He sent His Word and delivered me.

The Holy Spirit even prayed for me while I was sleeping one early morning. He used Psalm 6:1 (KJV): "O Lord rebuke me not in thine anger, neither chasten me in thy hot displeasure." The Spirit of the Lord also gave me the song, "The name of the Lord is a strong tower, the righteous run into it and is safe" (Prov. 18:10 KJV). The Lord set me free through His words and visions.

One night, with a loud voice, He said, "Touch not my anointed and do my prophet no harm" (Ps. 105:15 KJV). May we always rely on the Word of God and trust Him without a doubt. My God is good and merciful!

God saved my family from the spirit of death. An armed robber attacked my son. He went into his house and took all the money he had with him and his expensive phone. He also demanded the phone charger. While my son tried to look for the charger, the armed robber was also busy looking for other valuables to steal and did not realize when my son pounced on him and held onto the gun. As they fought, my son overpowered him, held him tight, and cried out for help until people came to his rescue. First responders called the police, and the armed robber was arrested. To God be all the glory for the great deliverance. Amen!

God restored the piece of land that belonged to my family. The enemy tried to claim our land we had since I was married for over fifty years, dating back to about three generations. His extended family tried to claim the land and would not allow us to use it, even when my husband was still alive. He made several attempts to peacefully settle the land dispute, but they refused.

In January 2021, my son called me that he was traveling home for the land case because they built a house foundation in our backyard and had also taken a large portion of our land. I told my son that the land dispute was over because the Lord Himself would redeem the land from the enemy. Prior to my son's plan to travel, I had a dream where I was given a paper to sign that the land dispute case was over, and I signed it. When I woke up from that dream, I believed that God had done it.

My son went for the land case on the last day, and they declared that the land belonged to my family, and the case was closed. Glory be to God!

I thank my Father for all the countless things He has done for me and my family. His deeds are marvelous and numerous. Truly, I cannot tell it all. Thank you, Jesus! Amen.

Comfort Okeke,
Wailing Women Worldwide

Chapter 12

God's Unfailing Love for Me!

I just want to praise the name of the Lord for His care, protection, provision, and sustenance toward my family and me. In October 2019, I was very sick. It all started with heart palpitations, for which I was hospitalized for two days. They did a lot of tests but could not identify the cause of the palpitations. All the blood tests and X-rays and magnetic resonance imaging (MRI) were normal, so I was discharged.

After being discharged from the hospital, I started having flaws and recurrent asthmatic attacks sometimes between two to three episodes a day. The doctor had previously given me an inhaler, so I used it. That was foolishness on my part. The attack continued on and off for eight days.

At this point, my husband decided it was time to go to the emergency room. I arrived at the hospital, checked in, and while I was waiting for triage, I started coughing intermittently. It felt like an eternity, but, at last, they called my name. While at triage, the attending nurse said to me, "You are having an asthmatic attack, and you are so calm." I said to myself, "So what am I supposed to do?"

After triage, I was assigned a room. Then came the technician to give me a nebulizer treatment. While he was setting up, the X-ray technician came in. They had to decide whether I should go for an X-ray or be nebulized. They agreed to send me for X-rays since it would only take ten to fifteen minutes. By now, it was probably around 8:00 p.m.

The hallway to the X-ray room was very cold. The X-ray was completed within the set time, and I was wheeled back to my room. Just as I was about to get up from the wheelchair to sit on the bed, I had another attack. This time, it was very bad that even in my confused state of mind, I heard the nurse say, "Oh my God. She is really struggling."

There was air everywhere, and everybody was freely breathing it, but I couldn't. It was as though both of my lungs totally collapsed due to the lack of oxygen.

My husband stood by my bed, and all he could do was pray and trust God for His intervention, and He intervened. It took a while for the nebulizer treatment to take effect, but amid the chaos, I felt the presence of God in that emergency room.

But for His grace and mercies that saw me through, they would have coded me that day. I was in the emergency room till about 3:00 a.m. for observation before I was discharged.

Once, I had to go to urgent care after the visit to the emergency room. For months, I kept up with a medication regimen, including a nebulizer twice a day, only leaving my home for doctor's appointments.

While all this went on, I was preparing to travel to Nigeria for my daughter's wedding. A friend said to me, "Patience, I know it's your daughter's wedding, but please don't go to Nigeria."

I had diligently prayed for this, so my response was, "Nobody is going to represent me at my daughter's wedding, so I am going." I went, trusting the Lord to keep me, and He did.

As much as I can remember, I have never been this sick my entire life. In retrospect, it seems like the devil was bent on taking my life, but God was keen on preserving it. Praise the name of our Savior Jesus Christ. God is faithful to His words: "Call upon me and I will answer." (Ps. 91:15 KJV)

I don't know what your needs are, but I know that if you continue to trust in Him, He will remove every care in the fullness of His timing. So, be encouraged. He did it for me, and He will do it for you in the name of Jesus Christ, our Lord.

Patience Erhiawarien,
Wailing Women Worldwide, USA

Part Three

GOD'S PROVISION

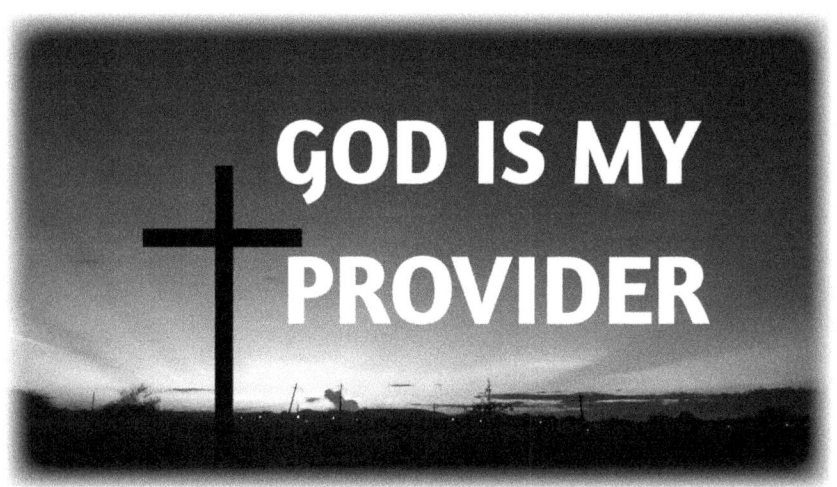

Chapter 13

God's Prophecy Fulfilled

"So shall My word be that goes forth from My mouth; It shall not return to Me void, But it shall accomplish what I please, And it shall prosper in the thing for which I sent it" (Isa. 55:11 ESV).

Vision through Dona Vauk – "Women in the shelter 2012."

Before the Pennsylvania National Conference in 2012, the Lord gave a prophecy to the Wailing Women Worldwide (WWW) USA secretary, Sister Dona Vauk, for Pennsylvania Wailing Women to invite women from the shelter and set a banqueting table and Pastor Stephanie Hicks to provide gifts to all the women and children.

The Lord connected us to a specific shelter through a sister who lived in the shelter some twenty years ago. After the conference, we continued the shelter visit every Sunday of the month. There were frequent movements and relocations of the residents, such that we could not follow up with what was happening to those women. It became a burden for me, especially for pregnant women.

Four years later, on October 22, 2016, we had the Tri-State Wailing Women Retreat in Cambridge Street, East Orange. At the end of the retreat, the Lord put fire in me to contact a sister who lived in Upper Darby, Philadelphia. This sister's information was given to me in 2012 during the conference in Pennsylvania, but we could not connect. My phone calls to her were unsuccessful, but she finally called back, and we arranged to visit the shelter in Philadelphia on Sunday, October 30, 2016, to share the vision of Wailing Women Worldwide.

After the shelter program, my husband and I, in the company of two other sisters, visited a sister and her husband (Daddy Moses) who lived in Upper Darby at their church. They took us to a restaurant, and we all ordered food. I was eager to share the vision of Wailing Women; I was not there for the food.

The couple told us, "Before you came, the Lord revealed you to us. The Lord wants to use you and your husband to facilitate his work. If Wailing Women is going from point A to point B, it needs logistics, and God wants to use you and your husband to facilitate the work. So, what do you want?" I told them we wanted a chapter of Wailing Women to be raised in Upper Darby, Pennsylvania, and we would like for her to buy into the vision of Wailing Women.

Daddy Moses said to me, "You are not listening! You think you came to raise a chapter, but that's not what God wants. God wants to empower you and your husband to do his work! So, what do you want?"

My husband was pinching me, so I told them about the burden to open a shelter, where the women would be ministered to and taught skills so that they could come out from the shelter, get their apartments, and be reabsorbed into the communities. For the Lord had laid in my heart strongly, "Just like Moses, what do you have in your hand? Use it!"

The couple asked, "So what are you waiting for?" I told them we did not have money to do any of that.

Daddy Moses asked, "Have you heard about 'no money down'?"

I told him, "No! That is a fairy tale."

He then gave a testimony of how he moved into his first house with no money down by using a postcard he picked up from the mail. He charged us to go home and register a business.

We went home and registered a business called Destiny Empowerment House of Hope. A week later, I prayed that I would also pick up something in the mail that would turn into money, just like Daddy Moses.

On that Monday, my husband picked up a postcard that had my name on it from one of these insurance companies for retirement benefits. Numerous phone calls ensured, and, all said and done, $15,000 was aggregated from two retirement accounts I was not aware I had funds. God surprised us with over $15,000 that we did not know existed. We were convinced that God wanted us to start the shelter and training of the women to become certified nursing assistants, but we did not know it took months to years of processing, accreditation, and licensing.

We had a last-minute disappointment in our attempt to buy a property and could not find another.

The couple in Philadelphia called us to come because they had a message for us. They told us that when Jesus went to Capernaum, He did not go straight. He made stops before He got to his destination. They told us that the shelter was the destination. The path to the shelter was home care. We ignored them and continued to search for a home, and it was unsuccessful.

One morning, the couple called and walked my son through the filling of an application that gave birth to Destiny Empowerment House and Groups LLC. The Lord himself ordered our footsteps each step of the way!

The couple called and informed us they would be out of the country on vacation. While they were away, I received a letter from the Pennsylvania Department of Health requesting some documents. I responded, not knowing I was in error. The couple applied for home care (non-skilled services), but my response was for home health (skilled services).

When the couple returned, we met with them to explain what had happened and how I responded to the department of health. They screamed, "OMG! You are not supposed to respond like that because we did not apply for home health."

We had to fill out another home care (non-skilled) application, and the couple told me to withdraw the home health application.

When we got home, I discussed it with our daughter Ginika, and God used her to direct my actions. She told me not to withdraw the application but leave it and watch. If it was the will of God, it would come through, and if not, so be it.

We were approved for home care (non-skilled) with accreditation for Medicaid services within a couple of months. And the home care was what held things together while the other arms of the business were processed. To God be all the glory!

I continued to process the home health application even after Daddy Moses and his wife told me to withdraw the application. The problem was I did not know what I was doing, and I couldn't go back to them to ask questions. So, I made up my mind to go with the flow, and whatever happened, so be it.

Destiny Helpers

We were blessed with various destiny helpers at the different stages of this project as enumerated below:

1. Help by an Unknown Medical Director

The department of health requested a medical director for the home health agency; we had no one to present. We had almost given up on that until 3:00 a.m. one early morning at Saint Michael's Emergency Department in Newark, New Jersey, and the Holy Spirit would have me look behind me as I sat at the nurses/doctors' station. As I looked behind me, it was laid in my spirit to go and ask the doctor if he would help us with that problem. I battled with it because the doctor did not live or work in Pennsylvania.

After much struggle, I went to him and explained to him our predicament. He told me he would help us. It turned out he had applied for a Pennsylvania license. He gave all his information for the completion of the requirements for processing. The problem of the medical director was miraculously solved by God. This was truly God!

2. Indian Woman Nurse – Equipment

One evening, I was working at Saint Luke's Emergency Department when an Indian woman who was also a nurse approached me and said, "So what do you do on the side?"

I was upset with the woman for asking me such a question. It was a very busy evening, and all I could think was, "Am I not doing enough, running around this emergency department drenched with sweat, for this Indian woman to have the audacity to ask me what I do on the side? So, I said to her with an attitude, "What do you do on the side?"

She giggled and said, "I am the regional inspector for the state of Pennsylvania. Anywhere there is a nurse aide program, I am the one the state sends to conduct the skill and written certification exam." My jaw dropped, and I immediately told her the vision to teach shelter women skills. She said, "Oh, that's easy! All you must do is gather equipment from the flea market; people donate medical equipment free, or if a wrong size of supply is opened for use in the emergency department, instead of them throwing it in the garbage, you should be collecting it."

She quickly went on the computer and printed a list of supplies needed for a nurse aide-skilled laboratory. She also asked me to register for training in Harrisburg, Pennsylvania, as a primary instructor.

She said, "As soon as you do all these, rent a room, gather five students, and I will come and test them." She further told me to have my husband go for training as the program coordinator. So, we registered and went for the three days of training. We were so lost in the training because we had no clue what they were saying! But we did get through.

3. Clinical Site – Caucasian Doctor

To start our training, we needed an approved nursing home as a clinical site. We went to all the local nursing homes, but they closed their doors to us. We were at our wit's end, ready to walk away from it. I went to work on one of the days, and a homeless woman came to the emergency department and was placed in my section. After the Caucasian doctor had seen the patient, he came out and asked who had the patient. I responded and said to the aide with me that the patient was homeless and would need shelter. He further said that if his wife was here, she would be all over this patient.

I said, "What do you mean?"

He said, "My wife runs around Allentown on Saturdays, delivering hot meals to homeless women."

I quickly shared the vision of women in the shelter and how God wanted me to train them and give them skills. The doctor said, "This is a noble course! Nurse aides are needed in health care. Good luck with it."

The next time I saw the same doctor was about three months later. He asked me how the school was doing. I told him, "Not doing."

He said, "Why?"

I told him all the local nursing homes had closed their doors, and we couldn't move forward. He told me to call up other nursing homes, make an appointment, and he would go with us.

On the day of the interview at the nursing home, he was with us. During the board meeting, he opened up and asked me to talk about the school and curriculum. This was how we ended up being approved for two clinical sites. The board of education came, inspected the school, and approved us.

4. Private School License – Unknown Woman

We needed to apply for a private education license to charge tuition. We planned to teach shelter women free and charge regular student tuition to be able to run the school.

We started the process of applying for a private education license. Our application was rejected three times, and we were to forfeit our money and start over again because we missed a deadline. My husband called the education license office and told them we lost my mother and had to take her to Africa for burial. They decided we had to put in an appeal.

On the day of the board meeting in Harrisburg, it was as if one was at the Supreme Court. My husband told them we were part of a ministry praying for this nation day and night, praying for the state of Pennsylvania. He told them how we would go to the shelter every last Sunday of the month and how God gave us this vision to empower the women in the shelter. The room was silent, attentive to what my husband was saying.

When my husband finished talking, they asked him what he wanted. He told them to give us a chance to redo the application and submit it before the next board meeting. They agreed to our request.

One week later, a woman called me and said that she would like to visit our school. She drove for two hours for the visit. She stated that she was in that room when my husband delivered his speech, and she was touched by that. She informed us that she had come to help us with the application and wanted to make sure we got the license. She worked with us and ensured that we got our license.

5. High Academic Goal – Professor Anigbogu

My first international leadership summit attendance was in the USA in February 2017. The theme of the summit was the **Birthing of the Midwives**.

This first leadership training was a boot camp, a military camp. After that meeting, I realized that though I was stretched like a rubber band, I couldn't break, and I could do all things through Christ who strengthened me. In Professor Vincent Anigbogu's words, "You cannot be stagnant; it's a dangerous thing! You must move with the times and seasons. You have to make yourself relevant." He noted that years ago, everything was done with paper. But today, everything is with the computer. Do not make yourself irrelevant by not moving with the changes.

Upon return from the summit, I decided to go back to school. By the special grace of God, I finished my doctorate degree in nursing practice (AGNP, DNP) in May 2021. I dedicate this degree first to God Almighty, who kept me through these years, and secondly, to Wailing Women Worldwide, who was the kick-starter through the summit training. And finally, to my wonderful husband for his unending support.

Conclusion

> The LORD had said to Abram, "Go from your country, your people, and your father's household to the land I will show you. I will make you into a great nation, and I will bless you; I will make your name great, and you will be a blessing. I will bless those who bless you, and whoever curses you I will curse; and all peoples on earth will be blessed through you" (Gen. 12:1–3 NIV).

In Abraham's calling, we see God's purpose, plan, and predestination. Abraham knew the destination of the journey. What he did not know was how to get there, how long it would take, and what would happen on the way to the destination. Not knowing the way, Abraham obeyed the call of God.

In his journey, Abraham faced famines, contentions between his herdsmen and his nephew Lot, jealousy between Sarah and Hagar, the problem of an heir, the war among the neighboring nations, and so on. Notwithstanding these, Abraham faithfully obeyed God's call because Abraham clearly knew the goal and believed that God would surely and successfully guide him until he arrived there.

We must take a step of faith to move when God says to move as our father Abraham. We have to give God something to work with, and God will perfect it. It is in those steps of faith that God shows up and shows off.

God asked Moses in Exodus 4:2, "'What is that in your hand?' 'A staff,' Moses replied." To Moses, it was just a staff used to beat stubborn sheep, but to God, it was an instrument by which miracles were performed.

My beloved brethren, what is that in your hand? We must give God something to work with. Do not make yourself irrelevant; stagnation is dangerous. Keep walking toward the plan and purpose God has laid out for you. Do not get distracted, and please do not stop. Keep running toward the eternal promise of God for your life. Amen!

Geraldine Anamege,
Wailing Women Worldwide, USA

Chapter 14

God's Unfailing Love and Faithfulness

"But my God shall supply all your need according to His riches in glory by Christ Jesus" (Phil. 4:19 KJV).

By the grace of God, I am an intercessor with the Wailing Women Worldwide-USA. With much gratitude and honor to the Lord God Almighty, my family and I feel blessed and humbled to return glory to God for His unfailing love and faithfulness.

About eleven years ago, my husband was doing his postgraduate medical education in a residency program. One night he had a dream in which he fell from a height into a three-story building and went through the floors onto the ground. When he hit the ground, it was like he landed on springs and automatically sprang up through the same opening created on his descent. Then he speedily ascended to a height higher than that from which he fell. From there, he could see the destruction caused on his way down. He was not sure about the meaning of the dream.

At the end of the academic year, the program director informed my husband that he would not renew his contract. Not understanding why this was, he responded by saying, "If it is the Lord leading you to do this, may His name be blessed." He was denied his end-of-year credits and certificate.

My husband moved on to obtain an additional qualification in the same field. After working for a while, he was told he could not use the license he had been approved for prior to the director's decision above. The sole breadwinner, my husband, lost his job.

Back home, we were faced with the issue of providing for the family. What would he do now? How would the family be sustained? There were too many questions with no ready answer. I could not imagine how he would handle this situation because nothing befitting his qualification or even near was on the table. During this period, one of us had to always stay home. With eyes full of tears, I suggested going out to get a job. He said to me, "My wife, I cannot stay home while you go out to work."

The doctor rolled up his sleeves with humility and faith in the Lord ("I know the thoughts that I think towards you, saith the Lord, thoughts of peace and not of evil, to give you an expected end" [Jer. 29:11 KJV]) and went to work with Amazon, where he packed boxes all night for one year. Amazingly, praise the Lord, God provided all our needs, and the family lacked nothing.

We were concerned about the situation but not worried because God was in control. He surrounded us with the right people: supportive wailing families. My wailing sisters, just four of us in the chapter then, took the matter personally. We fasted and prayed for three days and nights. The Lord responded through vivid dreams, and we held onto them. We also had the opportunity to have our then head national coordinator, Mommy Ebele, and national leaders, sister Lori and sister Oge, pray for us and over his documents. We held onto this prayer.

It is worth noting that our chapter was newly established at the time of the incident; not a coincidence, I am sure. The grace of God kept us peaceful, taking us through a situation that, in many cases, has led to broken homes, depression, and even death (murder or suicide).

Marveled by God's great love, I went on the Wailing Women Saturday testimony line to tell of His goodness. Hearing this, one of our national leaders, sister Yinka, asked me to call her later. She fervently prayed with us and for us and said, "It is well." We held onto that. We cannot forget this encouraging statement she made, "Thank God that you have a job you are not stealing."

From Amazon, my husband obtained a license and picked up a job as a truck driver with one of the local companies. He humbly and faithfully executed his duties despite many inconveniences.

A multitude of job applications and interviews yielded no fruit. All this went on for four years. We trusted God every step of the way and patiently waited for His time to come.

I spent most of my time on the prayer line, making sure I attended prayers on the general watch every morning. One day during my private prayers, I heard an audible voice speak out in my mother tongue, saying, "I heard yesterday." I looked around, and there was no one with me. Then I understood the voice I heard, and I held onto it. The Lord revealed many dreams to my husband, and we held onto them. We knew the Lord would do it, but how He would do it was not for us to understand.

One faithful day, my husband got a call with a job offer. Although it was underpaid, it was a step in the right direction. We were more than grateful to God.

Three months into this job, he was offered a new and higher position in the same establishment. It was a position he desired but could not get. It came at God's time with no effort. "For my thoughts are not your thoughts, neither are your ways my ways, saith the Lord, for as the heavens are higher than the earth, so are my ways higher than your ways, and my thoughts than your thoughts" (Isa. 55:8–9 KJV).

Today my husband is gainfully employed with responsibilities and compensation commensurate with his training. What more can we ask for? "Is anything too hard for the Lord? (Gen. 18:14 NKJV). "Now unto Him that is able to do exceeding and above that we ask or thinketh, according to the power that worketh in us" (Eph. 3:20 KJV). ***The Lord never fails. We must only believe.***

We thank God for all His willing and faithful servants He used along this journey. Our prayer is that God, who rewards those who diligently seek Him, will reward them.

Josephine Ngwang,
Wailing Women Worldwide, USA

Chapter 15

God's Miracle Gift

I had an old 1998 Ford Taurus that God miraculously gave me through His children—God's destiny helper—in March 2017. I was very thankful to God for it. Later, the car was having problems and was costing too much money to fix. I give glory to God for my pastor; he was instrumental in helping me fix the car.

I had a situation that required traveling for at least three to six months to take care of my granddaughter. I didn't want to continue paying insurance on the car since I would not be there for a while. So, I decided to give the car away. I thought of trading it in to get at least some hundreds of dollars, but I decided to give it out to whoever would need it, and it was given to someone who really needed a car in my church.

My next plan was to take care of my expenses for the Wailing Women USA national conference (flight ticket, accommodation, contribution to facilitators, etc.) and then save toward buying a new car. Little did I know that God was arranging another car for me through one of the Wailing Women sisters in my chapter. She lost her mother last year. Her mother left her and her brother a property, which they sold. She said God miraculously favored them by removing a very heavy tax that would have left them with little to no money on the sale of the property.

She was ready to give to God through her church. But God laid on her heart that "Grace needed a better-working car" and that she should give me the money for my car. She said the thought to buy herself a car didn't even come to her but to buy me one. She struggled with it and kept it within her heart for two months.

Finally, she was sure with confirmation that God meant what He said, and she made up her mind to buy the car for me. After that, she said that she felt joy and peace. In fact, the day she called to tell me, she was filled with joy and excitement. She gave me $10,000.00 for my new car. Hallelujah. Praise God.

Grace Folayan,
Wailing Women Worldwide, USA

Chapter 16

Trusting God

"Behold the fowls of the air. For they sow not, neither do they reap, nor gather into barns; yet your heavenly Father feedeth them. Are ye not much better than they?" (Matt. 6:26 KJV).

I am a living testimony! On February 3, 2020, while at work, I had a stroke that affected the right side of my body. The good Lord preserved my brain from destruction so that I can continue to praise and pray to Him. Although I forget very quickly, I have trust in God that He will surely rectify it at His appointed time.

I was very worried about how my family would survive, but the Lord reminded me how the birds don't toil, but the Lord feeds them anyway and how even the lilies in the field that don't spin nor toil, God allows them to grow and look beautiful.

Prior to the stroke, my husband had stopped working for over ten years, and we were content with the one income through me. After the stroke, the miracle-working God made my husband a home caregiver, and with the addition of my disability benefits and adjustments in insurance, we can pay for our bills and take care of orphans, widows, and the needy. The good Lord touched my children and the body of Christ to bless me repeatedly.

The Lord is restoring me; I can walk and move my hands. I am trusting God to heal my hurting left hand that disturbs me mostly at night. May the Lord continue to perfect all that concerns me and my family. "Heal me, Oh Lord and I shall be healed; save me, and I shall be saved, for you are my praise" (Jer. 17:14 KJV).

Veronica Akpan,
Wailing Women Worldwide, USA

Part Four
GOD'S DIVINE PROTECTION

The Lord
IS MY ROCK
MY FORTRESS
&
MY DELIVERER

Psalm 18:2

Chapter 17

My Grandchildren's Car Accidents

God delivered my two grandchildren from a ghastly accident in May 2017. A day before my grandson Michael's high school graduation, both of them were involved in a car accident in which their vehicles were written off, but they escaped with minor scratches. "The Lord shall preserve thee from all evil: He shall preserve thy soul. The Lord shall preserve thy going out and thy coming in. From this time forth, and even for evermore" (Ps. 121:8 KJV).

Ebun Adeyemi,
Wailing Women Worldwide, USA

Chapter 18

Supernatural Power of God

"Shouts of joy and victory resound in the tents of the righteous: The Lord's right hand has done mighty things! The Lord's right hand is lifted high; the Lord's right hand has done mighty things. I will not die but live and will proclaim what the Lord has done" (Ps. 118:15–17 NIV).

I love and serve the living God, who always watches over His children and all those who are His. My God is all-powerful and can quickly intervene in an impossible situation.

My God stepped into our lives and spared my family and me from premature death in February 2021 when a terrible snow and ice storm hit Texas. We should have all died from carbon monoxide poisoning, yet God did not allow it.

The electricity was shut off in my city of San Antonio, Texas, beginning early Monday morning February 15, 2021, at 2:30 a.m. My home was only getting electricity decreasing throughout the day in 10 minutes, 5 minutes, 3.5 minutes, and 1.5 minutes per hour. At 10 p.m. in the evening, the electricity was completely shut off for seventy-two hours (about three days) in frigid, below-freezing temperatures. The state of Texas was hit by two powerful snowstorm systems that made survival extremely difficult.

The temperature was twenty-two degrees below freezing outside, and the temperatures were also dropping inside our home. We had a gas stove, so we turned on the gas burners to have a heat source. However, we left it on for more than twenty-four hours and never turned it off. We did not know that we were not supposed to leave a gas stove on for such a prolonged period of time in an enclosed space. We were desperate for warmth and in shock that we would have been denied electricity when we needed it most.

By late evening, I was feeling sick and suffering from a headache and an elevated heart rate. My aunt Irene had also complained of a headache. However, I did not tell my brother Andrew or my aunt how sickly I was feeling. I went to bed to try and sleep that night, but I was worried and afraid. I have been sick to the point of death before, and this is what I felt.

I had not been able to think well all day nor concentrate on reading or prayer. I could not even formulate a prayer that entire day. I told God that I did not want to die like this. I offered to God a simple prayer and surrendered my fear and anxiety. I simply said, "If I live to see tomorrow, praise God. If I die, then I will see you soon, Lord." Then I fell asleep.

Our smoke alarm went off twice in the early morning hours. Both times, the alarm blared "Fire, fire." We checked the home, but there was no fire. The alarm was detecting the carbon monoxide from the gas stove and the candles we left on. We could have all died from carbon monoxide poisoning but for God's mercy.

Praise be to God that my aunt Irene, my brother, Andrew, and our cat, Jumpy, and I survived the night and made it to the next day. That day, Tuesday, my aunt's daughter, Jessica Castillo, called and urged us to leave our home and city and shelter with her family in the nearby town, for they had electricity and a warm home. We listened and left our home to shelter with our family and ride out the remainder of the snow and ice storms in safety.

My God kept us alive, and we all survived carbon monoxide poisoning. God also opened the right doors of favor so that we could shelter safely with relatives until our safe return on Thursday afternoon. My God supernaturally intervened in our lives and kept us from sure and silent death in the storm.

We could not save ourselves from our own ignorant mistakes. Only my God could save us by His supernatural power, strength, and might.

Praise be to the living God for saving us from a sure death!

Lucy Morales,
Wailing Women Worldwide, USA

Chapter 19

The Revealer of Secrets!

> "The king said to Daniel, "Surely your God is the God of gods and the Lord of kings and a revealer of mysteries, for you were able to reveal this mystery" (Dan. 2:47 NIV).

In 2021, I had two very bad dreams back to back, and I knew that Papa God was telling me that Satan was roaring. So, with the counsel of a man of God, my family and I immediately fasted and prayed for seven days. Our plan was to gather on the seventh day and give thanks unto the Lord.

On the sixth day of our fasting and praying, in the evening, Satan struck. One of my children was involved in a near-fatal motor vehicle accident. His car was totaled, but he walked away with no scratches or injuries. The two passengers in the other car also walked away without a scratch or injuries.

I remain loyal to the Revealer of Secrets and my Lover Jesus Christ, who reigns in my life and my family forevermore.

Dr. Okwuchukwukwuru Okpara,
Wailing Women Worldwide, USA

Chapter 20

The God of Impossibilities: With God, All Things Are Possible

"But Jesus beheld them and said unto them, with men this is impossible; but with God all things are possible" (Matt. 19:26 KJV).

Several years ago, one of my children who attended Boston College came home for vacation. On his flight back to Boston, as their flight was thousands of miles above in the clouds, the plane's turbine failed. An announcement was made for all passengers to brace for what appeared to be a disastrous and fatal journey. But my God made a way where there seemed to be no way. He flew into Boston on that plane with a failed turbine and landed smoothly. All passengers were unhurt. *What God cannot do does not exist.*

Dr. Okwuchukwukwuru Okpara,
Wailing Women Worldwide, USA

Part Five

GOD'S ALL-AROUND FAITHFULNESS

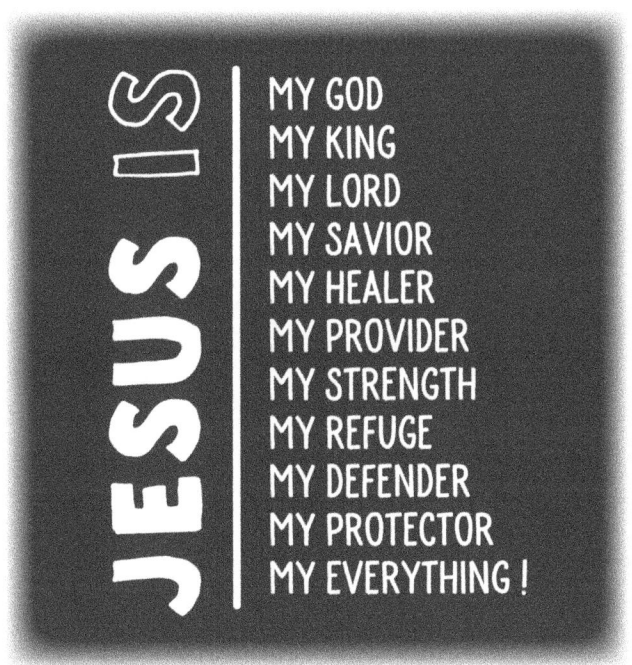

Chapter 21

My Daughter's Wedding

When I joined Wailing Women Worldwide, I had a burden in my heart. My second daughter was over thirty-five and not married. I prayed and asked the women to pray with me. I even posted the request on the WWW Facebook site with a pledge. In 2017, the conference was held in Arizona, and my daughter was still not married. So, I decided to pay my pledge ahead of the answer to my prayer by faith. "Let us hold fast the profession of our faith without wavering (for He is faithful that promised)" (Heb. 10:23 KJV).

I did, and it was counted unto me for righteousness. The Lord gave me a word to latch onto: **"the Zeal of the Lord of host shall perform it"** (Isa. 9:7b KJV, emphasis added). So I began to thank him in advance and started making wedding preparations. I also prayed with my daughter daily.

In December 2018, God orchestrated the meeting with my daughter's husband who came to visit from Australia. To cut the long story short, they got married in June 2019.

> "For the vision is yet for an appointed time, but at the end, it shall speak, and not lie: though it tarry, wait for it; because it will surely come, it will not tarry" (Hab. 2:3 KJV).

Glory to God!

Ebun Adeyemi,
Wailing Women Worldwide, USA

Chapter 22

YAHWEH God Comes to Town!

> "And we know that all things work together for good to them that love God, to them who are the called according to his purpose" (Rom. 8:28 KJV).

I left my past behind and headed to my new adventure in Bernalillo, New Mexico. Taking my heavenly Father with me in my suitcase instead of praying and asking Him to lead me and guide me, I took off for my eight-hour drive to my new home.

God has never failed me. Therefore, He met me in Bernalillo when I arrived. My new home was a three-bedroom, one-bath home on a corner lot. My friend helped me lay the carpet and tile and paint the home. Being new in the neighborhood, I had no friends or neighbors to help us, not even my son, who waved to us with a sweet smile of happiness while we worked. God sent His sweet spirit of peace that swept over our tired bodies.

Several months after settling into my new surroundings, I received a phone call from my friend. She informed me that the Lord told her to call me and let me know that He wanted me to organize a bike parade for the city of Bernalillo.

God had not told me to put on a bike parade, but I must be obedient to God's request because *I knew that God would lead, guide, direct, and make provisions for a successful bike parade.*

I did not know anyone, had no children, and had just started attending a church and had not developed friendships to help me with the parade. Is that not how God works? *With Him, we can do anything but fail.* I had the faith to believe that God makes the impossible possible.

I spent the next few months struggling with God's request to put on a successful bike parade. One hot night in August, while sitting at the edge of my bed praying for a cool breeze to blow into my window, I told the Lord, "Okay, but you must help me." The beautiful fragrance of roses came into my room. Yes, the God of heaven and earth was going to help me.

Parents were excited about the parade, and their children volunteered to participate as bike riders. The parents donated prizes for the children. The parks and recreation department provided valuable services for the parade and agreed to include us in their harvest in the fall activities.

I prayed. We needed a musician to usher in the presence of God. At that very moment, a beautiful fragrance of roses came into my room again. Yes, the God of heaven and earth was going to help me.

God always answers prayers. The following week, a new friend called me and recommended that I call a native man who played the drum, sang, and led worship in his native language. He asked for the route the bike parade would follow. I said, "From the north to the south."

He said, "That is prophetic; the Coronado soldiers of Spain came from the south into the ancient native pueblo and persecuted the native indigenous peoples. The children were walking from the north to the south. Their innocent blood had been felt cleansing and purifying the land because of the innocent blood that had been shed."

My heavenly Father told me that when I did the parade, He would do the rest, that it was a parade of reconciliation, forgiveness, and redemption. The blood of the innocent had cried out for justice.

On the morning of the parade, the weather forecast predicted a cloudy and very windy day. But the God of creation caused the day to be beautiful and no rain.

Three unusual incidences occurred after the parade: (1) during the night, two drug dealers had a shoot-out, (2) a family abruptly moved out of the city, and (3) a family was arrested for demonstrating violent behaviors toward others in the community.

Also, within one month after the parade, the crooked city mayor was ousted, and a new mayor was sworn into office that day. The new mayor promptly fired the city council and other city officials.

With the blessings from God, the heavens opened over Bernalillo, New Mexico, and the city became prosperous. Living conditions improved with the opening of new businesses, and the city flourished for the well-being and safety of the residents. Bernalillo, New Mexico, became a wonderful and blessed place in which to reside.

Deborah Romero,
Wailing Women Worldwide, USA

Chapter 23

A New Creation

"It is not the healthy who need a doctor, but the sick. I have not come to call the righteous, but sinners" (Mark 2:17 NIV).

"Therefore, if anyone is in Christ, the new creation has come: The old has gone, the new is here!" (2 Cor. 5:17 NIV).

Some years ago, I lived near a young man who was known in the neighborhood as a highly promiscuous person. I prayerfully approached him with the gospel of our Lord Jesus Christ. One day, I let him know that receiving Jesus Christ as the Lord of one's life is the best thing that could happen to anyone. I gave him my testimony of how I repented and decided to follow Christ without looking back, by His grace.

As time permitted, whenever we crossed parts, I chipped in things about the kingdom of God to him. Never did I condemn him of his immoral lifestyle because I knew he needed only to receive the seed of righteousness, and the Holy Ghost, our Teacher, would then convict and teach him the truth. I later got a job out of this city but within the same state and had to leave for my new job.

After some years, I went to get some documents from my former job. I met a man there who introduced himself as the former neighbor I had ministered to. He was excited and testified that he was a believer in Christ now and an ordained minister of the gospel in his present church. He added that his former girlfriend was now a believer. They both got married and started serving God together. He thanked me for sowing God's words and prayers in love in his life, all to the glory of our Lord Jesus!

Josephine Nwoko,
Wailing Women Worldwide, USA

Chapter 24

Wailing Women Worldwide: A Gift from God!

I joined Wailing Women Worldwide around April 2019 after relentless multiple invitations from a precious sister with Wailing Women Maryland, USA.

In June 2019, I was privileged to attend the USA Wailing Women National Conference in Maryland. As the hosting state, members were assigned to transport our international mothers to the conference venue upon their arrival in Maryland. Mama Princess was one of the mothers I had the opportunity to ride with.

During this drive to the hotel/conference venue, a conversation came up that compelled me to mention that I had joined the group approximately three months previously. I remember Mama Princess told me that I would not regret joining Wailing Women. She further said something to the effect that "Wailing Women Worldwide is the last bus stop." Little did I know how intensely this phrase would impact my walk and work with the Holy Spirit. It was as if the Holy Spirit had been patiently waiting for me to join the Wailing Women for Him to unleash His instructional package for me. Now and then, I will hear the phrase "**the last bus stop**."

After the conference, I was blessed with leaving the conference venue in the same car as Mama Gift. I do not know how the Holy Spirit did it, but Mama Gift visited me in our house, shared some kingdom secrets with me, and prayed over a couple of bottles of olive oil for me.

Several months later, the Holy Spirit instructed me to take one of those 500ml bottles of olive oil to a designated place in our state and empty the whole bottle at once. He supplied grace and courage to get it done.

When I joined Wailing Women, I was informed that Wailing Women USA was on a 24/7 prayer chain for the family, nation, and church, and that every member was expected to be on the 5:00 a.m. EST general watch and join any other hour. I made up my mind to join either 9:00 or 10:00 p.m. when I was done with work and family time/dinner. I love my sleep way too much to join any hour from 11:00 p.m. to 5:00 a.m. However, the Holy Spirit had a different plan.

While I was sleeping at night, I felt myself suspended in the air right above my bed, gently being rocked back and forth on what felt like an invisible hammock. I opened my eyes and wondered what was going on with me and if my sugar level was too low. I got up to check my sugar level, and it was normal. I went back to sleep, and the same thing happened again, but this time, I felt compelled to get out of bed and go down to our family prayer room.

Getting there, I was prompted to call the Wailing Women prayer line. When I did, the 3:00 a.m. watch was just calling in, and, of course, I ended up praying with them. A similar incident happened around the same time on the second and third day. In summary, the Holy Spirit assigned me to the 3:00 a.m. watch.

There are so many other specific things and dealings that have been made available to me by the Lord that may not be mature enough for me to testify at this time. An undeniable fact is that being under the umbrella of Wailing Women Worldwide has transformed not just my spiritual life but my family and work life.

Everything about me seems to undergo a daily transformation, and I have found myself praying for the grace to keep up with the Lord and Wailing Women. I am thankful that our international mothers provided us with training manuals, the mandate, and the operational handbook. I am humbly and sincerely grateful for the gift of Wailing Women to me, my family, and humanity as a whole.

Calista Uzuegbu,
Wailing Women Worldwide, USA

Chapter 25

Incredible God: I Stand in Awe of Him!

"For the LORD Most High is AWESOME, the Great King over all the earth" (Ps. 47:2 NIV).

My third son, a junior lawyer at a firm in Houston, Texas, received a call on March 8, 2021. The caller introduced himself in the message and informed my son that his profile "popped" up on some kind of platform. A law firm had seen it and wanted to interview him. My son thought it was a gimmick because he did not apply for a job, had never heard of the platform, and had no plans of even looking for a new firm. So, on March 9, 2021, my son returned the call. It was no gimmick. He was interviewed on March 11, 2021. Three hours later, he was offered the job. He went from junior to senior lawyer, a bigger and better law firm, and a thirty-thousand-dollar increase in salary.

Dr. Okwuchukwukwuru Okpara,
Wailing Women Worldwide, USA

Chapter 26

God's Faithfulness

"I sought the Lord and he answered me" (Ps. 34:4a NIV).

On July 1, 2019, during the Wailing Women annual conference in Maryland, our mother in the Lord, a prophetic woman of God, totally sold to Jesus, Sister Yinka, had a revelation. Her revelations were accompanied by intervals of melodious music from the choir she simultaneously conducted. She prophesied that by "next year," some of our children would get married, and in nine months, there would be "baby cries" in many homes.

The conference room got so quiet you could hear a pin drop. My eyes started blinking nonstop as my heart pondered over her words and wondered at the possibility. Could she be referring to me? Was God about to grant my heart's desire? I ran with those questions.

Yes, I did remember Mommy Ngozi Ojefua's words, **"God will always be God in all situations."** It was true. I knew my son was in a serious relationship that could lead to a union. I believe in prophetic words and always speak positively about them. I quickly claimed Sister Yinka's prophecy and agreed with the mandate from our international mother, Mommy Uche. She advised us to declare Psalm 127 over our family daily.

My mind never got off that revelation as I continued to declare Psalm 127. The marriage happened, and that intensified my thinking about the revelation. The fulfillment of the revelation came to pass in 2020 despite COVID-19. A bouncing baby boy was delivered to my family to the glory of the Almighty God.

The revelations have increased my faith and spiritual growth. This also confirmed the truth in the song, "Trust and Obey" (John H. Sammis).[4]

To God be the glory!

Dr. Florence Okpala,
Wailing Women Worldwide, USA

---

[4] Sammis, John H.,"Trust and Obey", 1887

Epilogue

Thrilling Testimonies: You Shall Testify

"He hath made every thing beautiful in his time: also he hath set the world in their heart, so that no man can find out the work that God maketh from the beginning to the end" (Eccles. 3:11 KJV, emphasis added).

The God of Wailing Women Worldwide is still in the business of saving, healing, and delivering people from sin, affliction, disease, death, and so on. Our sincere prayer is that as you have read through these testimonies, you will be encouraged and inspired to seek God for yourself in a personal and intimate relationship. "And blessed *is* she that believed: for there shall be a performance of those things which were told her from the Lord" (Luke 1:45 KJV).

Nothing is impossible for our God. Whatever situation or difficulty you are now encountering, you can come to God and ask Him for help and intervention. All you have to do is cry out to Him for help. He hears our heart cries, and He sees our tears. Just reach out to Him in prayer and supplication regarding your trial, tribulation, or storm. He has declared in His Word that in this life, you shall have trouble, but for all of us to take heart because He has overcome the world.

Release and hand over that situation to the Lord, and watch what He can do in your personal trial. Watch the Lord work that situation out in His own special way as He did with every contributor to this book. There is no need to worry, be anxious, or stress over your particular situation, for God will work it out for His glory and for your good.

In the end, you can thank Him and then testify of the goodness of the Lord in the land of the living. And perhaps you will join the chorus of the many voices in this book and be one of the many thrilling testimonies of this good, good God who never ceases to amaze us with His protection, provision, and guidance. This amazing, living God is always at work doing the miraculous in all of our lives.

> "Now unto the King eternal, immortal, invisible, the only wise God, be honour and glory forever and ever. Amen" (1 Tim. 1:17 KJV).